Easter

The
Greatest
News

PAUL WILLIAMS

Easter
The Greatest News

10 Publishing
a division of 10ofthose.com

Copyright © 2021 by Paul Williams

First published in Great Britain in 2021

British Library Cataloguing in Publication Data
A record for this book is available from the British Library

ISBN: 978-1-913896-04-1

Designed and typeset by Pete Barnsley (CreativeHoot.com)

Printed in Denmark

10Publishing, a division of 10ofthose.com
Unit C, Tomlinson Road, Leyland, PR25 2DY, England

Email: info@10ofthose.com
Website: www.10ofthose.com

1 3 5 7 10 8 6 4 2

Contents

Introduction

The door

I remember very little about my childhood, but there is one moment that is indelibly imprinted in my memory because it was truly traumatic.

It happened when I was in the second year of secondary school – Year 8 in today's currency. The entire year group were lined up in a school corridor, in alphabetical order. We were waiting to be ushered in, one by one, into a small room – the nurse's office. Every pupil in the year was waiting – silently, nervously, like lambs to the slaughter – to be given a BCG injection.

The BCG is an inoculation against the disease tuberculosis, which attacks the lungs. TB, as it is commonly known, is a killer. It was once responsible for one in eight of all deaths in the UK. Even today, it's still a terminator –

worldwide, 1.5 million people died of the disease in 2019.

I was oblivious to those alarming statistics as I stood, quietly, as a twelve-year-old boy. Being a 'W' (Williams), I was almost at the end of the line, but by taking one small step to my right and craning my neck around the other pupils in front of me, I could see one kid after another go through the door marked 'Nurse'. As I watched the first few anxious kids go in and out of that room, it wasn't long before I witnessed an event that sent a shiver down my spine and left an imprint on my mind like an image caught on camera.

It involved a lad called Nigel Bailey. (Though, actually, I have changed the names in this account to protect the identity of all involved – and to ensure I don't get sued for libel!) Anyway, Nigel was one of the toughest boys in the year. You didn't get on the wrong side of Nigel Bailey – not if you were fond of the current arrangement of your face.

Nigel disappeared into the nurse's office. When he came out, just moments later, I had the fright of my life. Nigel Bailey emerged looking like death warmed up. This tough lad – the hardman of Year 8 who could reduce any of us to shivering wrecks with one of his menacing stares – walked out of the nurse's office looking as white as a sheet. All the blood had drained from his face. As he made his way back towards the classroom, he staggered along the corridor. Like a man who'd spent the night knocking back tequilas, he was unable to walk in a straight line. He swerved along the corridor, passing all the other kids in the queue. Then, as he neared the end of the line, just a few metres from me, his ghostlike complexion changed. Like a chameleon, he began to turn 'green'. He put his hand over his mouth, picked up his pace – bumping into Mike Waters in the process – and ran as fast as he could, making a beeline for the door to the playground, where he promptly threw up.

It was a horrible moment. Admittedly, it wasn't great for Nigel Bailey, but it was truly terrifying for me. I thought to myself, 'If that's what happened to Nigel Bailey in the nurse's office, then there is no hope for me.' From then on, I was really scared. If that injection had reduced hard-as-nails Nigel Bailey to such a pathetic specimen of humanity, then I was certainly going to die in there! I went weak at the knees, began to shiver and at the same time felt hot under the collar. And I was not the only one. My good friend Neil Turner turned around and stared at me with a look that said, 'We are toast!'

So as I stood there, getting more and more nervous, I decided to fix my eyes on another lad halfway up the line: Peter Harris. I could see Peter easily. Everyone could see Peter easily. He was the tallest boy in the year. For some reason his somatotropin (growth hormone) had gone into overdrive years ahead of all the other kids in the year, so he stood head and shoulders above everyone else in the line. But Peter was also the skinniest boy you would ever see. He looked like a bamboo shoot – tall and thin, with the occasional knobbly bit sticking out.

Focusing all my attention on beanpole Peter, I figured that if he could go through the door marked 'Nurse' and come out again alive, then maybe I could survive it too.

Peter Harris did get in and out of that door unscathed. The moment he emerged, alive and well, I had great confidence that I too could enter the nurse's office and live to tell the tale. The fact that I'm writing this book, forty-six years later, tells you that my confidence was not misplaced. Clearly, I *did* survive the BCG injection. Looking back now, as I retell the story, I realise it all sounds rather melodramatic. But I recount it to illustrate a problem that cannot be exaggerated in its gravity. A problem that most of us don't care to talk about. A problem that's not going to go away by ignoring it. A problem that every one of us will have to face one day. I'm thinking about the terrifying truth that one day all of us will have to go through a door marked 'death'.

No human being can escape this problem of death. Due to the worldwide coronavirus pandemic, with its staggering death rate, every one of us has been confronted by it more sharply than in any of the previous seventy-five years since the end of the Second World War. The bare fact is that even the toughest, most successful, wealthiest and most self-confident people who walk planet earth have to face the door marked 'death' sooner or later.

Of course, we're not literally standing in line waiting to walk through that door, but the chilling truth is that every day each one of us takes a step closer to reaching that place. It's a petrifying prospect. The thought of going through that door and never coming back hangs over us all our lives.

However, that is precisely why Easter is the greatest news we could ever hear – because Easter tells us how we can enter that door with confidence.

Easter is about a man in history who towered above everyone else who has ever walked this planet. This man went through that door marked 'death' and then actually came out again – alive.

Easter tells us that if we fix our eyes on that one man, we too can walk through the terrifying door of death with total assurance that everything is going to be OK. More than OK. Easter means that death can be the doorway to the beginning of the most wonderful experience of our lives.

Hang on, though – I'm getting way ahead of myself. First, I need to tell you the whole story of Easter.

1

The sign

Do you have a hero or heroine from history? If so, who is it? There have been some remarkable people who have graced this planet. What human being would you call the GOAT – the Greatest Of All Time?

- William Shakespeare, the literary genius?

- Blaise Pascal, the philosopher?

- William Wilberforce, who is often credited with abolishing the slave trade?

- Ludwig van Beethoven, the composer?

- Mahatma Gandhi, the leader of the Indian Independence Movement?

- Emmeline Pankhurst, the suffragette?

- Albert Einstein, the scientist?

- Winston Churchill, the wartime Prime Minister?

- Rosa Parks, the civil rights activist?

- Nelson Mandela, the anti-apartheid campaigner?

Some of the great people of history have had greatness thrust upon them. Some have wanted none of it. Others have revelled in the adoration they received as a result. Some have claimed remarkable things for themselves.

I have no idea whether Jesus Christ would come close to being your greatest hero of history, or whether he'd even make it into your top ten. But there's no doubt that he's had a huge impact on the history of the world. Just look at today's date. It is over two thousand years since the birth of Jesus Christ. He marks the start of what we now refer to as the Common Era (CE).

I find it astonishing that the majority of the 7.5 billion citizens of the world measure time from the days when Jesus walked planet earth. His existence has had such a profound effect on humanity that the whole of time has been split in two: CE and BCE (Before the Common Era). All years are either before Christ (BCE) or since Christ (CE). That means that every day when we refer to the date, our lives are lived in reference to Jesus.

So why did Jesus have such a huge impact on the world? The Christian claim is that he is none other than God himself. It is an assertion of the most momentous proportions. Christians believe that God came and walked this planet. Christians maintain that this astonishing claim is substantiated by the events of Jesus' life.

This is the launchpad for what happened at Easter and for the greatest news we'll ever hear. The first thing we need to grasp is that Jesus of Nazareth was no ordinary man. He was a man, a flesh-and-blood human being – and we need to be clear on that – but he was so much more. That's what Peter, one of the first men to follow Jesus, declared. This short book about Easter looks at one of the first Christian sermons ever preached – by Peter.

Peter was a fisherman who met Jesus one day while going about his day job. We can read all about the encounter in Luke's Gospel, chapter 5 and verses 1–11. Peter (also referred to as Simon Peter or Simon) had been on the night shift, but might as well have stayed in bed. He had spent all night on the sea, but he and his workmates had caught nothing. Zip. Zilch. The fish just weren't biting – not that he fished with rods, lines and hooks. He'd been out in his boat all night with his nets down and hadn't caught a thing – not even a tiddler. So he and his companions had rowed back to the shore, where Peter had got down to the laborious business of washing the nets. Then Jesus, a carpenter who'd become an itinerant preacher, turned up on the beach and started preaching to a crowd of people who had gathered around him. Jesus was so cramped by his audience that he decided to borrow Peter's fishing boat and use it as a kind of floating platform. He asked Peter to push it a little way out to sea, sat down in it and preached from there. Then, when he'd finished his 'sermon', he told Peter to row to deep waters and let down his nets again.

As Peter had just washed the nets following a frustrating and fruitless night's fishing, it's remarkable that he didn't simply ignore Jesus or sarcastically ask this carpenter-cum-preacher what he knew about fishing. Maybe because of Jesus' preaching or something of Jesus' already burgeoning reputation – though we don't know exactly why – Peter followed Jesus' instructions. Peter and his fellow fishermen rowed out to sea, threw their nets overboard and 'caught such a large number of fish that their nets began to break.'[1] That was the beginning of it all for Peter. He was hooked! Convinced that Jesus was someone special, Peter left his fishing business and started to follow Jesus.

What Peter witnessed in the years that followed proved that the fishing miracle was no fluke. Jesus performed one miracle after another, including more miracles on the water. On one occasion, Jesus stilled a terrifying storm. Peter and some other followers of Jesus were convinced they were going to drown, but Jesus calmly stood up and told the wind and waves to be still. Instantly – yes, instantly – the storm stopped. The sea became as smooth as a millpond on a warm summer's day. On another

---

1. Luke 5:6 (that is, Luke's Gospel, chapter 5 and verse 6).

occasion, Jesus walked across a deep lake. Yes, you did read that correctly – he walked on water.

Then there were Jesus' miracles with food and drink. At a wedding, when all the wine had run out, Jesus turned gallons of water into the finest wine – wine that would have graced the cellars of Fortnum and Mason. On another day, when a huge crowd of well over five thousand people had gathered to listen to Jesus speak, they began to get hungry. Out in the countryside, and with no McDonald's around the corner, Jesus turned a young lad's packed lunch (a couple of fish and a few loaves) into a feast that fed and satisfied everyone in the crowd – with basketfuls left over.

Then there were miracles of health. Jesus gave blind people their sight. Lame people were able to walk after meeting Jesus. Sick and dying people were cured.

Any one of Jesus' miracles would leave your jaw dragging on the floor in sheer wordless wonderment. But perhaps the greatest wonders were the literally death-defying miracles. People who were dead were brought back to life by Jesus. And Peter saw it all.

However, it wasn't just Peter who witnessed these incredible events. Nor was it only Jesus' other followers who observed and then attested to the astonishing events. These nature-defying, laws-of-science-eluding, life-reversing miracles were seen and experienced by thousands of people. That meant that Peter could say these words, as he preached to several thousand people in Jerusalem:

Fellow Israelites, listen to this: Jesus of Nazareth was a man accredited by God to you by miracles, wonders and signs, which God did among you through him, as you yourselves know (Acts 2:22).

In effect, Peter said to the crowd that Jesus has been shown to be more than a man by the miracles he did. Then, crucially, Peter told his massive audience that these miracles were done 'among you', 'as you yourselves know'. The miracles of Jesus were seen by many, many people.

If we'd been born two thousand years ago, at the very beginning of the common era, and had we lived in Israel, we'd have been able to see these miracles with our own eyes. Jesus' miracles were not done hidden in a corner, or in a specially designed film studio with clever but deceptive camera angles.

Just take arguably the greatest miracle of them all – the resurrection of a man called Lazarus. Lazarus had been dead for four days. His flesh had already begun to rot, which is why the mourners feared there would be a terrible stench if the tomb was opened. Lazarus was well and truly dead. And yet, with a word of command, Jesus called this dead man out of his tomb, and Lazarus came out. People were there when this happened. They saw Lazarus shuffle out of the tomb, with his grave clothes still wrapped around his body. In the following days, what a story Lazarus must have told. I can imagine he became a most coveted after-dinner speaker. Our guest tonight is 'The man who came back from the dead'.

Jesus did mighty miracles to demonstrate that he was more than a mere man, and the general public saw the miracles with their own eyes.

One of the big questions people have about Christianity is a basic but most crucial one: 'How do you know God exists?' Here is the answer. We know God exists because two thousand years ago he came and walked planet earth, and he made perfectly clear who he was by the miracles he performed.

I'm a Christian minister, so you won't be surprised to hear that I've been asked many times to 'prove' the existence of God. I say something like this: 'When Jesus walked planet earth, he did things that were out of this world to show that he was from out of this world.'

Some people reply to my answer with, 'Ah, the miracles of Jesus. You don't expect me to believe that they happened, do you?'

But let me ask you this. If God were to walk this earth, what would you expect him to do? If someone were to approach *me* and say, 'I'm God,' I'd say, 'Prove it.' If they couldn't do anything to prove their claim to be God, I'd put them on a par with someone who claimed to be William Shakespeare! The miracles of Jesus are precisely what we'd expect God to do if he graced this third planet from the sun.

Jesus' public, miraculous ministry is very good news if we're looking for evidence for the existence of God. But it's also very important if we're to understand Easter. Jesus is the man who is God, and he demonstrated this by the life he lived among us. It's astonishing. What we hear next is scandalous.

2

The scandal

My social media feed regularly features footage of wounded or trapped animals being rescued and released by kind human beings. It's remarkable the lengths people go to save helpless animals that would otherwise die a slow, agonising death. An almost universal feature of those videos is that when the animals are first approached by their rescuers, they react with fear. That fear is often expressed in the animal aggressively attempting to hurt their rescuer. Wild animals assume that humans approach them only in order to have them for dinner!

The Easter story features human beings lashing out in a similar way against the One coming to save them. The first surprise is that the One who came to save humans was their

Creator. The second surprise is that, unlike the animals who resist in order to protect themselves, our resistance has no acceptable explanation. Indeed, we discover in the events of that first Easter that we are more wicked than most of us have ever imagined.

In chapter one, we saw that the evidence of Jesus' life and the miracles he performed show that he is God. Given his life of tender compassion and wonderful justice, you'd have thought that we humans would have welcomed the most loving man who ever lived. You'd have thought we'd have hailed him on the world stage as one to follow and emulate. You'd have thought we'd have tried to follow his teaching and his example in an attempt to make this world a better place. What actually happened was quite different, as Peter explained next as he addressed the crowd in Jerusalem:

This man [Jesus] was handed over to you by God's deliberate plan and foreknowledge; and you, with the help of wicked men, put him to death by nailing him to the cross (Acts 2:23).

Let me spell this out so that we understand just how shocking it is.

God came among us, lived the most beautiful life, stood up against unjust and corrupt leadership, gave women a voice, and gave all men a mission in life. He told us the meaning of life and offered deep-down, joyful life for all eternity. He demonstrated that he was God by his miracles … and humans murdered him. We put him to death in the cruellest form of execution known to man at the time. Hung on a cross of wood, he suffered a most humiliating, degrading and painful death. Humanity should have hailed him, but instead, we nailed him to a Roman instrument of torture, until his final breath was squeezed out of him and his heart stopped beating.

How scandalous that humanity would treat God like that. It begs the question, 'Why?'

Not so long ago, I was chatting to a guy called Roger – a nice fella; a decent, hard-working bloke. Roger said to me, 'The problem with Christianity is that it's so … restricting. It cramps my style with, you know, "Thou shall not do this, that and the other." I don't want anyone telling me how to live my life.' Then he asked, 'What right does God have to tell me what to do?'

Strangely, because of the coronavirus pandemic, I reckon we understand the answer to Roger's question better now than we ever have. If I'd told you in the autumn of 2019 that within six months we were going to be ruled by a government that insisted we stayed at home – and that we would only be permitted to leave our home to go to work (if that was essential), or to get medical assistance, or to buy food, or to exercise once a day – I doubt you'd have believed me. If I said that all restaurants and bars would be closed by the government, and – wait for it … that they were slapping fines on people who didn't comply, I wouldn't have believed it myself. If you did think that my extraordinary suggestion was even a vague possibility, you'd have imagined that we were going to be invaded, and then occupied, by a totalitarian regime led by a ruthless and wicked dictator.

However, in the spring of 2020, as we went into lockdown and lived through the unprecedented restrictions placed on us by the government, most decent citizens not only complied with those restrictions but actually agreed with them. Why? We understood that the government's rules were for our good, the good of the many and the good of the most vulnerable.

We can't draw a perfect parallel, but I refer back to those lockdown restrictions to illustrate that God is no tyrant when he tells us how to live. He acts for our good. When he says 'no', it is in order to bless us and not to harm us – like a good father refusing his little children access to the kitchen drawer where the knives are kept.

My friend Roger's concern is that God is a restrictive God – one who keeps telling us 'no' and as a result takes all the fun out of life. In fact, the one true living God is not primarily a God of restrictions at all. The 'Thou shall nots' that Roger felt so restricting are far from the whole story – they don't even tell the majority of the story.

The God of the Bible is loving and astonishingly generous, kind and giving. He's far more of a 'Thou shall' God because he has given us freedom of choice, having generously created for us a beautiful and spectacularly good world in which to live.

Consider the wonderful world he has created. One writer admits:

I have very little imagination. If it had been me [creating the world] I think I'd have made one kind of tree and some grass and maybe some flowers too and then gone off for a rest. God did a bit better than that. He made thousands of kinds of grass, and not just one kind of fruit tree but pears and plums and peaches and pomegranates – and that's just a few that begin with 'p'.

Think of all the flowers too – red poppies so delicate they fall to pieces if you pick them, daffodils like gold, sweet peas that can fill a garden with Chanel No 5.[2]

The wonder of creation tells us not only of God's power and precision, but also of his generosity, kindness and love. Think of all the good things we enjoy in this life: friends, fun, food; sand, sport, skiing; relaxation, romance, recreation. God is a generous God. He wants us to enjoy life.

---

2. Julian Hardyman, *Glory Days* (IVP, 2006), pp. 21–22.

So when he does tell us not to do something, it's for our good; for our protection; for the good of society; and for the good of the vulnerable. When God tells us how to live, he is *for* us.

Strangely, though, we don't like that. As Roger put it, 'I don't want anyone telling me how to live my life. What right does God have to tell me what to do?' God gives us everything – including giving us life in the first place and then giving us every breath we take. We want all the good things God gives us, but we want him to butt out.

Our attitude is remarkable. At best we ignore God. When two thousand years ago he came among us to rescue us, he so cramped our style that humanity killed him. Wanting our independence, we declare war on God. We make him our enemy. Though God gives us every good thing we enjoy, we don't want anything to do with him, except on the occasions when it suits us.

So when God turned up on earth, we humans got rid of him because we didn't want anyone telling us how to live our lives – not even God. We want to live our lives our way. You don't need me to tell you what a terrible thing that is to do, but thankfully there's another side to the Easter story.

3

The plan

I love looking at images that can be seen in two different ways. Here's a couple. [3]

In the first one, you can either see a saxophone player or a woman's face. If you're having trouble

---

3. Source:
https://www.exploratorium.edu/brain_explorer/double.html

seeing the woman, it may help to know that the little cloud below the saxophone player's nose is the woman's left eye (seen to *your* right). The second is a picture of a rat or a man with glasses. The rat's ears become the man's glasses. The tip of the nose is the same for both. These types of images are great fun when you get them, but maddening when you don't.

Similarly, the death of Jesus on a cross on the first Good Friday can be seen in two different ways. There are two sides to the Easter coin.

In the last chapter, we saw one side. One reason Jesus died on a cross was because we human beings didn't want God telling us how to live our lives, so when he showed up, we wanted him out of our lives and off the planet. But there's another side to the cross. A glorious side. The death of Jesus on a cross was all part of God's plan for the salvation of the world.

Listen again to the words of Peter:

This man [Jesus] was handed over to you by God's deliberate plan and foreknowledge; and you, with the help of wicked men, put him to death by nailing him to the cross (Acts 2:23).

It was God's set purpose that Jesus should be handed over to be crucified – a plan made before Jesus came to Jerusalem; before he started his public ministry; before he was born in a stable; before the angel visited Mary announcing Jesus' birth. Long before all that, there was a preconceived plan that Jesus would die on a cross to rescue us from rebelling against God.

Although we kick God out of our lives and deserve his punishment, that's not the end of the story. God loves us and therefore went to the most extraordinary lengths to restore our relationship with him. He doesn't just make the first move; he makes the second move and the third and the fourth and … God makes all the moves to repair the relationship that we ruin. The decisive move happened on that first Easter weekend as Jesus died on a cross. In many ways, it was the culmination of all God's moves!

Most people I meet want to live in a just and fair society. We don't like even a hint of injustice or corruption in our legal system. When a jury is unable to convict a felon; or a mistake is made by the prosecution and someone who is irrefutably guilty gets off on a technicality; or a judge gets it all wrong by dishing out a lenient sentence: when those things happen, there is an outcry. We don't like injustice; we want justice.

What we want in society, we want of God too. We can't bear the thought of God not being just and fair. People have often said to me, 'I won't follow a God who doesn't do anything about …' Then they cite an appalling atrocity in history or in the recent news. The good news is that God will punish evil. That's why there is a place called hell, where evil is punished. God would not be a loving God if he didn't do so. It would be wrong of God to let wickedness and evil go unpunished. The bad news is that this wickedness includes you and me.

When I first looked into Christianity, it dawned on me that I had committed the greatest crime in the universe. I'd rebelled against the God of all creation who loved me. Largely, I didn't want anything to do with him. That same animosity towards God drove people to crucify Jesus on that first Easter. Yet even though Jesus' death looks like a disaster, it was – as we have already said – all part of God's plan.

Despite the appalling way we've treated God, he, in his glorious love, wants to restore our relationship with him. He wants to be our friend. But here's the problem: he can't just let us off. That would not be just, and we want justice. So, motivated by his astonishing love and in order to act justly, God did the most remarkable thing imaginable. To spare us the punishment that we deserved, God took that punishment himself:

[Jesus] was handed over ... by God's set purpose and foreknowledge; [....] to death [...] on a cross (Acts 2:23).

In your mind's eye, come with me to a courtroom. There's the judge on the bench. There you are, in the dock. The sentence is being passed. You're guilty. You've rebelled against God. The punishment is life imprisonment. In this justice system, 'life' means 'life'. You are never to be released. As the sentence is passed, you're devastated, but you don't have a leg to stand on. This is justice. Since you're guilty, you are receiving what you deserve for crimes against divinity.

Then imagine the judge steps down off the bench and stands next to you in the dock. He looks at you and says, 'While you deserve your punishment, because I love you, you can go free. I'm going to serve your sentence for you.' For a jaw-dropping moment, you stand there unable to believe your ears. Then relief floods over you. You feel your heart pounding as the prison guards cuff the hands of the judge and then lead him off to serve your life sentence. You are free to live the rest of your life. You are acquitted and declared not guilty.

That's a little picture of what Jesus did for us. Our sentence was death – eternal death. God couldn't just let us off – that wouldn't be just. Yet because God loves us, he sent his Son Jesus to die for us. Jesus took our place, according to God's set purpose. That was the divine reason for Jesus' crucifixion and why Good Friday is such good news for us. And that's how it's possible for us to enter with confidence that door marked 'death'.

Jesus died for our sin, taking the punishment we deserve, so we could be forgiven. Jesus' death can make us ready to meet our Maker, having been forgiven, acquitted and found not guilty. It's the best news we could ever hear. But just when you thought it couldn't get any better, it does.

4

The victory

'I'm not afraid of death; I just don't want to be there when it happens.' So said the actor, comedian and Hollywood director, Woody Allen.

His fascination with death combined with his wit makes him very quotable. On another occasion, he quipped, 'I don't want to achieve immortality through my work; I want to achieve immortality through not dying.'

In a more serious moment, he admitted, 'All men fear death. It's a natural fear that consumes us all.'

Some people tell me they're not frightened of death, but in thirty years of Christian ministry, I have only ever met one man who lay on his death bed and refused to listen to the possibility of life after death. Even then, his wife (soon to be his widow) was terrified for him.

Few people are genuinely fearless of death, whether it's the prospect of nothingness – of just not existing anymore; or not knowing what's waiting for us, or the possibility that on the other side there is a terrible judgement to come. That's why Easter Sunday is such a brilliant day.

Two thousand years ago, on what we now call 'Good Friday', Jesus Christ went through that door marked 'death', only days later to burst out of the grave on Easter Sunday, alive and well. On Easter Sunday Jesus Christ defeated death.

This is what Peter next declared to the crowd:

God raised him [Jesus] from the dead, freeing him from the agony of death, because it was impossible for death to keep its hold on him (Acts 2:24).

Later in his sermon, Peter said,

… he [Jesus] was not abandoned to the realm

of the dead, nor did his body see decay. God has raised this Jesus to life (Acts 2:31–32).

For me, because we all have to face death, this is the greatest news in the world. A real flesh-and-blood man has gone through the door marked 'death' and come out again, alive and fighting fit. It changes everything.

We deceive ourselves by thinking that we can stop or prevent death. Last year, the oldest man in England became the oldest man in the world at 112. Asked the secret of his long life, he joked, 'I've avoided dying!'

People have been trying to avoid dying since the beginning of time. Many of us try to put off that fateful day by exercising regularly, taking vitamins, eating healthy food and doing everything in moderation.

From the moment we take our first faltering steps, our loving parents protect us from and teach us how to avoid death. They erect stair gates so we don't kill ourselves falling down the stairs. They put plastic covers over the plug sockets so we don't electrocute ourselves.

They tell us to look both ways before crossing the road. They give us handy life tips like not poking a knife in the toaster and never playing with fireworks.

For the mentally stable, death is something to be avoided. Some, however, go to extreme lengths, spending a small fortune in an attempt to avoid the inevitable. The 'science' of cryogenics takes bodies at the moment of death and freezes them at temperatures below -150°C. Individuals pay for this believing that in the future when medical science has made further advances, their frozen body will be thawed out, brought back to life and then 'cured' of whatever finished it off in the first place. Some will go to extraordinary lengths to hang on to life.

Perhaps you are tempted by the idea of being frozen, but even if there were spectacular medical advances, it would still only delay the inevitable. That's why it's so astonishing that Peter could say that death could not keep its hold on Jesus. Jesus was raised to life, never to die again. A human being has beaten death once and for all.

Woody Allen will never gain immortality through not dying, but the life-changing message of Christianity is that with Jesus Christ we can die and then experience immortality – real flesh-and-blood everlasting life. Who wouldn't want that?

About twenty-eight years ago, I met a man who said, 'I don't want to live forever.' It really took me aback.

At the time, I'd just been visiting a member of the church family who lived in a nursing home. Thelma was a delightful, positive Christian lady. Whenever I went to see her, I'm sure I gained far more from the visit than she did from seeing me! As I left Thelma's room and walked through the nursing home's communal area, I was feeling uplifted by my time with her. The sun was shining too. In my chirpy state of mind, I caught the eye of an old man sitting on a chair and looking out of the window. 'Alright?' I asked.

In a grumpy voice, he replied, 'No.' It stopped me in my tracks.

'Oh,' I said. 'Can I get someone to help you?' I presumed he needed some nursing assistance.

'No-one can help me,' came the gruff reply.

I pulled up a chair, introduced myself and asked the old man his name. Then Bert began to tell me that no-one ever visited him, he was in pain most of the time, he had nothing to look forward to and he just wanted to die. My heart went out to him. I asked him if I could tell him the good news of Jesus – how Jesus could give him life forever. That was when he stated, 'I don't want to live forever.' It took me by surprise because it was the first time that I'd ever met someone who so blatantly declared that they didn't want eternal life. I'd met plenty of people who didn't want to know about Jesus, but even they hoped for something good after death. I was lost for words.

Then Bert explained. 'Why would I want my life to go on forever?' he asked, since he was in so much pain and all the enjoyment of life had been sucked out of him years ago. His bold assertion made sense.

If life after death is anything like the life he was experiencing now, he didn't want to live forever – he'd rather just die and bring it all to an end. Why would you want life to go on forever if eternal life is a constant struggle with pain and disappointment?

That's *not* the promise of eternal life that Jesus offers. The resurrection of Jesus doesn't simply extend this life forever. That could be misery. For some, it would be torture. Jesus was raised to *life* – not just existence. The Christian gospel teaches that eternal life is a joyful, fulfilling, abundant life with the God who made us and loves us more than we could ever imagine. That's Peter's meaning when he quoted Psalm 16 in Acts 2:28:

> *You have made known to me the paths of life;*
>   *you will fill me with joy in your presence.*

The eternal life that Jesus Christ offers is a life of joy forevermore.

Think back to the best day you ever had – the 'perfect' day. That day when the sun was shining and you were with the person or people who mean the most to you in all the world. That day when you didn't have a worry in the world. The day you never wanted to end. Then imagine it never did end.

That might give you just a glimmer of the eternal life that we're talking about here. That's what the resurrection of Jesus Christ puts on offer. I know it seems too good to be true, but it's not.

5

The evidence

It was two days before the end of the spring term and the beginning of the Easter holidays. I had been asked to speak at an assembly at a private girls' school. I must admit that, as I drove to the school, I was more than a little nervous – for two reasons. First, I was going to be standing in front of five hundred teenage girls. Second, I was going to eat a daffodil! Yes, you did read that correctly – I was going to eat a real daffodil.

You won't be surprised to hear that I'd not done that before. In fact, you might be quite relieved to hear that I wasn't (and still am not) in the habit of consuming flowers. But I knew it could be done, having nicked this idea for a school assembly from an older minister. He'd eaten a daffodil and lived to tell the tale. So, as

I drove to the girls' school, I was also excited at the thought of giving them an arresting, memorable and hopefully unforgettable school assembly. Let's face it, school assemblies are rarely very exciting for the pupils, but I reasoned that eating a daffodil would be sure to grab their attention.

The rather prim and proper headmistress introduced me as 'The Reverend Paul.' I stood in front of the girls and took a yellow daffodil out of a vase that I'd previously positioned on the table at the front of the hall. Without saying a word, I began to eat the daffodil, petal by petal. 'Uuugh!' 'Yuuuck!' Nervous laughter! It was certainly getting a reaction – and not only from the girls. My tastebuds were responding in rebellion. It was as if they were screaming at me, 'What do you think you are doing? STOP IT! Are you out of your mind?'

The experience was revolting, but I was committed to it. With a thousand eyes staring at me, I couldn't stop now. Every 'mouthful' took a huge effort to swallow, but I persevered. Even though it seemed to take forever, I finished off the daffodil. Then I made my point: 'Girls, if you go home today and say to your parents, "A vicar came into assembly and ate a daffodil," your parents might not believe you. But if ten or fifteen of you all told your parents the same thing, they might begin to believe you. Although,' I conceded, 'they might think you'd got together and made up the story.

'But,' I continued, 'if your parents met all five hundred of you over the next few days and you all told them the same fact – a vicar ate a daffodil – the sheer volume of eye-witness evidence would substantiate the claim.'

Then I read these words from a letter that Paul, one of Jesus' followers, wrote:

For what I received I passed on to you as of first importance: that Christ died for our sins according to the Scriptures, that he was buried, that he was raised on the third day according to the Scriptures, and that he appeared to Cephas, and then to the Twelve. After that, he appeared to more than five hundred of the brothers and sisters at the same time, most of whom are still living, though some have fallen asleep. Then he appeared to James, then to all

the apostles, and last of all he appeared to me
also (1 Corinthians 15:3–8).

Do you see Paul's point? He states it clearly: more than five hundred people saw the risen Jesus. Not just one or two individuals. Not a dozen or fifteen witnesses. But more than five hundred. What's more, these words were written just twenty-five or thirty years after Jesus' death and resurrection, therefore most of those who saw the risen Jesus were still alive at the time. So, had we been the first recipients of Paul's letter, we could have found these eye-witnesses and spoken to them – even 'interrogated' them if we felt that way inclined. We could have investigated this bold declaration for ourselves.

The resurrected Jesus was seen on different occasions and by hundreds of people including Peter and his companions. As Peter told the crowd:

God has raised this Jesus to life, and we are all
witnesses of it (Acts 2:32).

The bodily resurrection of Jesus is based on the evidence of solid, reliable eye-witnesses. I find this wonderfully reassuring.

Years ago, when I was discussing Christianity with a bloke called Greg, he said, 'I'm not going to rip my brains out and flush them down the toilet.' He was a straight-talker! He thought Christianity was all an elaborate fabrication to make weak people feel better about life.

What I admired about Greg (apart from his straight-talking) was his willingness to engage with a position on which he didn't agree. Over the months that followed, Greg took time to intellectually consider Christianity. He didn't rip his brain out but kept it very definitely switched on, as it should be. As he carefully worked through all the evidence, Greg became convinced that the bodily resurrection of Jesus Christ was incontrovertible. He became a follower of Jesus.

To follow Jesus is the next logical step – for Greg and for all of us – because if Jesus really, historically and bodily rose from the dead, then:

- Jesus is God as he claimed.

- We know God exists.

- Jesus' death on the cross can bring forgiveness.

- Jesus' death can reconcile us to God.

- Jesus has defeated death.

- Jesus can give us eternal life.

If all this is true, then someone *has* gone through the door marked 'death' and come out the other side. Furthermore, if we connect ourselves to him, then he can give us life beyond the grave too.

The eye-witness evidence for the resurrection is compelling, but there's more – something you might find even more astonishing.

6

The prediction

Fanatical fans of *The Simpsons* will know that this American animated sitcom has a reputation for having correctly predicted the future! From Donald Trump becoming President to the discovery of the Higgs boson particle, to a major plot twist in the highly acclaimed *Game of Thrones*, apparently, you could have heard it first on *The Simpsons*!

Personally, I'd put that down to the scriptwriters making a few lucky guesses or having a bit of insider information. However, just imagine if someone could *actually* tell you what was going to happen in the future – not just next week or next month, but hundreds of years from now. Imagine someone wrote down detailed predictions and then, centuries later, they came to pass with unerring accuracy.

Peter said that's the case with the resurrection of Jesus. It was predicted hundreds of years before it happened.

In his sermon, Peter quoted from the Old Testament book of Psalms:

David said about him [Jesus]:

'I saw the Lord always before me.
 Because he is at my right hand,
 I will not be shaken.
Therefore my heart is glad and my tongue rejoices;
 my body also will rest in hope,
because you will not abandon me to the realm
of the dead,
 you will not let your holy one see decay.
You have made known to me the paths of life;
 you will fill me with joy in your presence'
(Acts 2:25–28).

This extract from Psalm 16 was written by one of Israel's former rulers, King David, about a thousand years before Christ's birth on earth. As

Peter explained, while David was the author of this psalm, he couldn't have been writing about himself because he, David, died:

> *Fellow Israelites, I can tell you confidently that the patriarch David died and was buried, and his tomb is here to this day. But he was a prophet and knew that God had promised him on oath that he would place one of his descendants on his throne. Seeing what was to come, he spoke of the resurrection of the Messiah, that he was not abandoned to the realm of the dead, nor did his body see decay (Acts 2:29–31).*

This is astonishing. A thousand years before it happened, King David predicted the resurrection of one of his descendants. Now, Peter declared, that prophecy has been fulfilled. Even the sceptic must surely concede that while any of us could predict a resurrection from the dead, it's quite another thing to pull it off!

I could make a case for that one fulfilled prediction being evidence enough to convince anyone to give at least some serious time to investigating the claims of Christianity. However,

I don't need to rely upon just that one fulfilled prediction because there were many, many more prophecies fulfilled by Jesus Christ at Easter.

Psalm 22 was also written by King David – again, around a thousand years before Jesus. The psalm begins:

My God, my God, why have you forsaken me?
(verse 1).

If you've ever engaged with Easter events, those words might ring bells. They are the words that Jesus cried out as he hung on the cross (see Matthew 27:46). While Jesus choosing to echo words that had been written hundreds of years beforehand is not remarkable, what is incredible is how the detail in the rest of the psalm was fulfilled at the scene of the cross. Psalm 22 describes with remarkable accuracy the events surrounding Jesus' death:

All who see me mock me;
    they hurl insults, shaking their heads.
'He trusts in the Lord,' they say,
    'let the Lord rescue him.

Let him deliver him,
    since he delights in him' (verses 7–8).

Those words were hurled at Jesus by the religious leaders as they watched him die (see Matthew 27:42). Jesus may have deliberately chosen to quote the first line of this psalm, but getting those who hate you to quote from a psalm to make your case is quite another matter.

Verse 16 reads:

… they pierce my hands and my feet.

That's a remarkable description of how Jesus was actually executed. Yet, once again, those words were written hundreds and hundreds of years earlier.

Verse 18 says:

They divide my clothes among them
    and cast lots for my garment.

As Jesus was being crucified, his Roman guards – who would have known nothing of these Jewish psalms – did exactly this with his clothing (see Matthew 27:35).

The detail of the prophecy of Psalm 22 is astounding. A thousand years before Jesus' crucifixion, and before that barbaric method of capital punishment had even been devised, the actions of independent people at the scene of the crime had been predicted.

As Jesus cried out the first line of Psalm 22, 'My God, my God why have you forsaken me?' I reckon he was doing so for two reasons. First, because that's what was happening on the cross: Jesus was being cut off from God the Father so that we don't have to be. Second, in order to draw our attention to the whole psalm, showing us that the manner and details of his death had been predicted with unfailing accuracy a millennium before it happened.

Psalm 22 and Psalm 16 are just a few of the many fulfilled predictions in the Bible about Jesus' life, death and resurrection. I suppose a few prophecies coming true could be put down to pure chance, but there are dozens of examples of specific prophecies being fulfilled in Christ.

While you can't (and shouldn't) believe everything you read on the internet, a simple Google search 'Prophecies fulfilled by Jesus' will point you to scores of examples. Many things in the Old Testament (the part of the Bible written before Jesus) were then fulfilled in and by Jesus. The probability of them all coming true by chance is gargantuan.

A Professor of Mathematics and Astronomy, Peter W. Stoner, has calculated that the chances of just eight prophecies coming true by sheer chance are 1 in 10 to the power of 17 (100,000,000,000,000,000). He calculates, 'That would be equivalent to covering the whole state of Texas with silver dollars two feet deep and then expecting a blindfolded man to walk across the state and on the very first try find the *one* coin you marked.'[4]

Whatever you make of that probability statistic, I find the fulfilment of all these prophecies of Jesus both astonishing and reassuring. Jesus' death and resurrection were predicted, in meticulous detail, hundreds of years before they happened. As we saw earlier,

---

4. https://bit.ly/3dMRL61

Easter was part of God's deliberate plan and foreknowledge.

Added to the eye-witness evidence, we have good reason to believe the events of that first Easter really can bring us forgiveness and life beyond the grave. The question is how do we gain these for ourselves?

7

The reaction

I was twenty when I began to seriously investigate the claims of Christianity. When I first understood the great news of Easter – that my sin could be forgiven at the cross and that Jesus had defeated death through his resurrection – I jumped at the chance of knowing this forgiveness and having eternal life.

About three thousand people in the crowd listening to Peter had the same reaction (see Acts 2:41). As Peter recounted:

When the people heard this, they were cut to the heart and said to Peter and the other apostles, 'Brothers, what shall we do?' (Acts 2:37).

When I first looked into Christianity for myself, I became very aware of my failings and faults. I became convinced that the biggest 'sin' I had committed was that, like the people who nailed Jesus to a cross, I wanted God out of my life. Many of those who first listened to Peter felt the same about how they had treated Jesus. God had come to earth and yet they wanted him out of their lives and off the planet. Cut to the heart, they wanted to know what to do.

Peter replied:

Repent and be baptised, every one of you, in the name of Jesus Christ for the forgiveness of your sins. (Acts 2:38).

In those words, Peter explains how it is possible to be forgiven and to have a restored relationship with God.

1. Repent

To 'repent' means to 'change your mind'.

When the truths of Easter grab our hearts, we realise we need to transform the way we think. We need to change our mind about:

- Who Jesus is.

- What place God should have in our lives.

- How we have rejected God.

- What we most want in life.

- For what we are going to live.

Changing our mind will change the way we live.

On a car journey, have you ever taken a wrong turn and found yourself driving in the complete wrong direction? Once you've realised your mistake and acknowledged that you are going in the wrong direction, you turn around as soon as you can.

In the same way, repentance is a change of mind that results in a change of direction in life. Repentance is the first step to becoming a follower of Jesus.

2. Be baptised

When a person is baptised, they are plunged into water as a sign of cleansing and reviving.

We use water every day for two things: to wash and to drink. Water cleans us and keeps us alive.

Water in baptism is a sign – or a picture, or a visual explanation – of what Jesus does for us. Through his death on the cross, Jesus cleanses us from our sin and brings us forgiveness. Through his resurrection, Jesus defeated death and can give us eternal life.

For the believer, baptism is an outward sign and declaration that we have trusted in Jesus for our forgiveness and for the gift of eternal life.

We connect ourselves to Jesus by repenting and being baptised. Then we can be sure of eternal life.

Being joined to Jesus is like a thread that is connected to a needle. When we start sewing, everywhere the needle passes, the thread follows. When we repent and believe in Jesus, we are connected to Jesus; everywhere he goes, we follow. He died and rose again, so though we die, we will rise again. Jesus went through the door marked 'death' and came out again, so we too will emerge from death, alive forevermore.

However, before we die and experience glorious joy in the presence of God, there's a wonderful gift given to us. As Peter continued to state:

> *Repent and be baptised, every one of you, in the name of Jesus Christ for the forgiveness of your sins. And you will receive the gift of the Holy Spirit (Acts 2:38).*

The Holy Spirit is God's Spirit, who is given to everyone who truly repents and believes in Jesus. This is wonderful news.

The Holy Spirit living in you means that God's presence is with you all the time. No matter where you go, God is with you.

Being a follower of Jesus is not easy. Of course, it's completely worth the cost – just think about an eternity with him – but that doesn't make you popular. However, even when you feel rejected, you are not alone. God is with you.

What's more, the Holy Spirit gives us his power to live differently. It's one thing to want to live for God, but quite another having the resources to do so. The gift of the Holy Spirit means that you are no longer living your own life your own way, but are empowered to live for God.

Receiving the Holy Spirit doesn't mean we instantly become perfect, but his presence with us does change us so that, over the years, we become more like the person we should be. We become more like Jesus.

Forty-six years ago, I was terrified about walking into that door marked 'Nurse'. Four years later, my best friend tragically walked through the door marked 'death'. Lawrence's death was utterly life-changing for me. As a teenager, I was slapped around the face with the devastating truth that I was not indestructible. The day that Lawrence died brought me to a realisation that many people have grasped, whether through the death of a friend or a loved one, or the thought of their own death: left to ourselves we have no answers to the problem of death.

But a few years after Lawrence's tragic death, wonderfully, my brother told me how the Easter events could make me ready to go through the door marked 'death'. Jesus' death and resurrection mean that we can walk through that door with the total assurance of coming out the other side into glorious, joyful, eternal life in a beautifully restored relationship with God.

Easter guarantees an eternity full of joy in God's presence.

If you can think of any greater news, I'd love to hear it.

8

The response

Thanks for reading this little book. Having considered what I've described as the greatest news anyone can hear, I hope you're asking yourself, 'What should I do next?' Here are a few suggestions:

- If you write to me (my address is below), including your postal address, I'll send you a free copy of Luke's Gospel. This Gospel is a carefully investigated, eye-witness account of the events of Jesus' birth, life, death and resurrection. I can also do my best to recommend a good church near you.

- Join a Christianity Explored Course,

where you'll be able to ask any questions and learn more about Jesus and the claims of Christianity. You can search for a Christianity Explored course near you here: https://www.christianityexplored. org/Groups/276341/Find_a_Course. aspx?redirected=1

If you would like to start following Jesus, here is a prayer you could say:

Heavenly Father, thank you that you love me so much that you want to rescue me.

I admit that I have turned away from you, not living my life for you. I see how wrong that is. Today I repent of wanting you out of my life. Thank you that I can be forgiven because of Jesus' death on a cross. Thank you that Jesus' resurrection gives me the assurance that I can be with you forever when I die. Please give me the gift of your Holy Spirit so that I can know your presence with me always, and so that I can be empowered to live for you from now on – until I am finally with you forever for all eternity. Amen.

If you say that prayer, then let me urge you to follow the three steps above so that I can send you a copy of Luke's Gospel and help you find a church, and then you can find a Christianity Explored course.

Paul Williams
c/o 10ofthose
Unit C, Tomlinson Road
Leyland
Lancashire
PR25 2DY
England

email: info@10ofthose.com

Epilogue

The speech

This little book has been shaped around the words of Peter, one of Jesus' first followers. Peter's speech, as we have it in the Bible, is:

Fellow Israelites, listen to this: Jesus of Nazareth was a man accredited by God to you by miracles, wonders and signs, which God did among you through him, as you yourselves know. This man was handed over to you by God's deliberate plan and foreknowledge; and you, with the help of wicked men, put him to death by nailing him to the cross. But God raised him from the dead, freeing him from the agony of death, because it was impossible for death to keep its hold on him. David said about him:

'I saw the Lord always before me.
      Because he is at my right hand,
      I will not be shaken.
Therefore my heart is glad and my
tongue rejoices;
      my body also will rest in hope,
because you will not abandon me to the realm
of the dead,
      you will not let your holy one see decay.
You have made known to me the paths of life;
      you will fill me with joy in your presence.'

Fellow Israelites, I can tell you confidently that the patriarch David died and was buried, and his tomb is here to this day. But he was a prophet and knew that God had promised him on oath that he would place one of his descendants on his throne. Seeing what was to come, he spoke of the resurrection of the Messiah, that he was not abandoned to the realm of the dead, nor did his body see decay. God has raised this Jesus to life, and we are all witnesses of it. Exalted to the right hand of God, he has received from the Father the promised Holy Spirit and has poured out what you now see and hear. For David did not ascend to heaven, and yet he said,

'The Lord said to my Lord:
   Sit at my right hand
until I make your enemies
   a footstool for your feet.'

Therefore let all Israel be assured of this: God has made this Jesus, whom you crucified, both Lord and Messiah.

When the people heard this, they were cut to the heart and said to Peter and the other apostles, 'Brothers, what shall we do?'

Peter replied, 'Repent and be baptised, every one of you, in the name of Jesus Christ for the forgiveness of your sins. And you will receive the gift of the Holy Spirit. The promise is for you and your children and for all who are far off – for all whom the Lord our God will call.

Acts 2:22–39